The Complete Soup Maker Cookbook

1200 Days of Delectable and Gratifying Soup Maker Creations for All Machines Using Metric Measurements and Local Ingredients to Delight Your Tastebuds | Full Color Edition

Sharron B. Malec

Copyright© 2024 By Sharron B. Malec Rights Reserved

This book is copyright protected. It is only for personal use. You cannot amend, distribute, sell, use, quote or paraphrase any part of the content within this book, without the consent of the author or publisher.

Under no circumstances will any blame or legal responsibility be held against the publisher, or author, for any damages, reparation, or monetary loss due to the information contained within this book, either directly or indirectly.

Disclaimer Notice:

Please note the information contained within this document is for educational and entertainment purposes only. All effort has been executed to present accurate, up to date, reliable, complete information. No warranties of any kind are declared or implied. Readers acknowledge that the author is not engaged in the rendering of legal, financial, medical or professional advice. The content within this book has been derived from various sources. Please consult a licensed professional before attempting any techniques outlined in this book.

By reading this document, the reader agrees that under no circumstances is the author responsible for any losses, direct or indirect, that are incurred as a result of the use of the information contained within this document, including, but not limited to, errors, omissions, or inaccuracies.

Editor: AALIYAH LYONS

Interior Design: BROOKE WHITE

Cover Art: DANIELLE REES

Food stylist: Sienna Adams

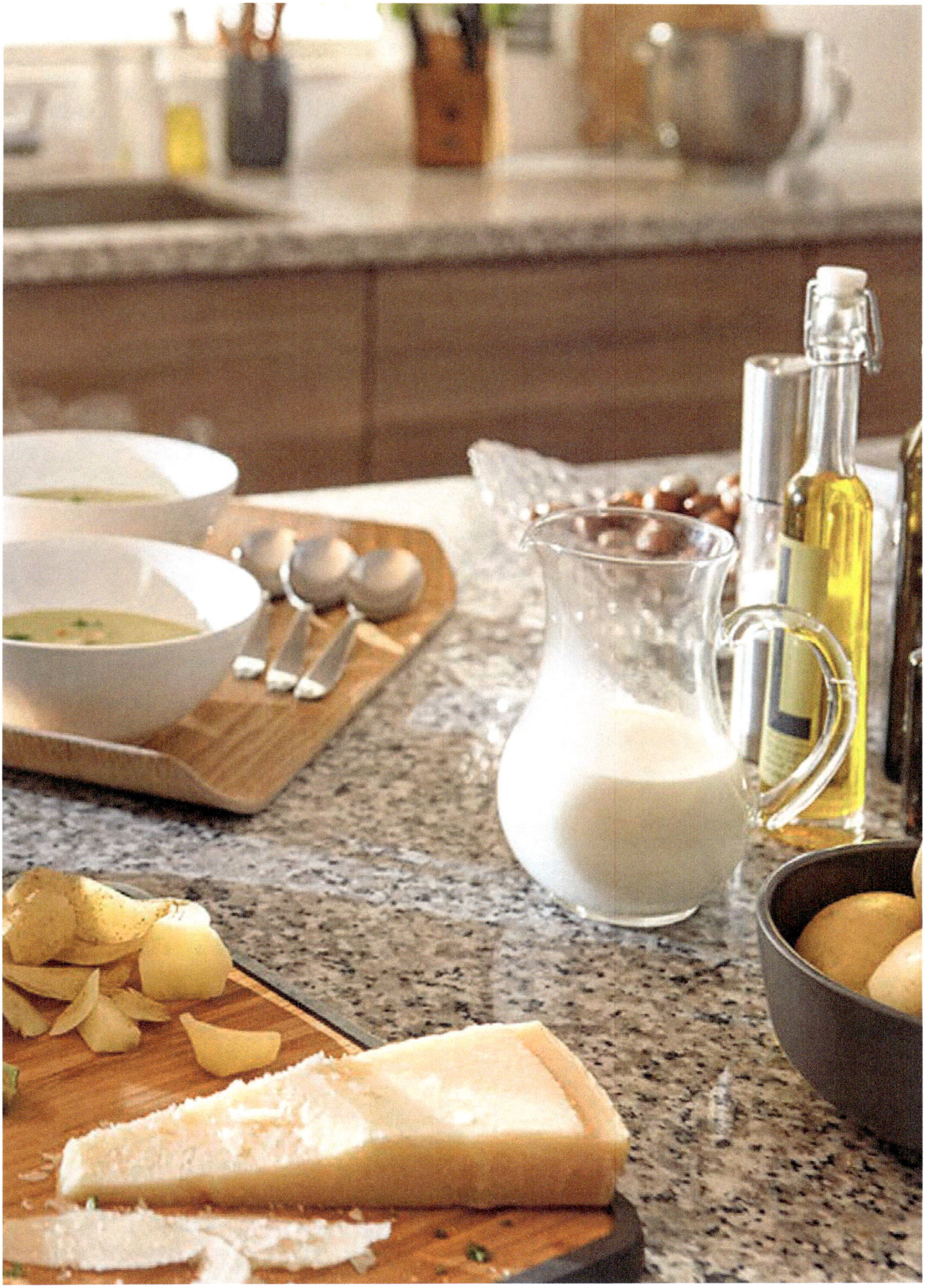

Table Of Contents

Introduction	1	Chapter 3	
		Grain, Beans and Lentils Soup Recipes	10
Chapter 1		Pasta and Bean with Basil Oil Soup	11
Embark on Your Soup-Making Odyssey	2	Seasoned White Bean Soup	11
The Soup Maker Revolution Unveiled	3	Broad Bean and Mint Soup	12
Tips for Soup Maker Mastery	4	Winter Lentil and Vegetable Soup	13
The Art and Science of Soup Making	4	Mexican Lime, Bean and Tomato Soup	13
		Mexican Bean Soup	14
Chapter 2		Healthy Chickpea Split Pea Soup	15
Stocks and Broths	6	Hearty Lentil and Vegetable Soup	15
Rich Beef Broth	7		
Classic Chicken Stock	7	Chapter 4	
Vegetable Stock	8	Poultry Soup Recipes	16
Mushroom Broth	8	Top Turkey and Wild Rice Soup	17
Fish Stock	9	Red Bean Turkey Soup	17
Turkey Bone Broth	9	Chicken and Anellini Pasta Soup	18

Cauliflower Chicken Soup	19
Chicken and Sweetcorn Soup	20
Turkey and Bacon Soup	21
Classic Chicken and Asparagus Soup	21
Turkey and Vegetable Quinoa Soup	22
Sweet Potato and Thai Chicken Soup	22
Chicken, Carrot and Corn Soup	23
Hearty Turkey Noodle Soup	23

Chapter 5
Meat Soup Recipes — 24
Beef Stock and Onion Soup	25
Pork and Cabbage Stew	25
Lamb and Chickpea Soup	26
Italian Spicy Sausage and Pepper Soup	26
Hearty Beef and Vegetable Soup	27
Beef and Vegetable Soup	27
Lamb and Barley Soup	28
Pork and Bean Soup	28
Bolognese Beef Soup	29
Venison and Root Vegetable Stew	29
Tomato and Sausage Soup	30
Chunky Beef Stew	30

Chapter 6
Bacon and Ham Soup Recipes — 31
Ham and Potato Soup	32
Bacon Squash Soup	32
Ham and Pea with Crispy Bacon Soup	33
Old English Pea and Ham Soup	33
Sweet Potato and Bacon Soup	34
Smoky Ham and Lentil Soup	34
Beer Cheese and Bacon Soup	35
Easy Ham and Broccoli Soup	35

Chapter 7
Fish and Seafood Soup Recipes — 36
Curried Cod Cauliflower Soup	37
Coconut Milk and Fresh Crab Soup	37
Haddock and Sweetcorn Soup	39
Smoked Salmon Cabbage Soup	40
Garlic Mussels and Plum Tomato Soup	41
Hearty Salmon and Vegetable Soup	42

Chapter 8
Vegetable Soup Recipes — 43
Spring Greens and Asparagus Soup	44
Spicy Sweet Potato and Peanut Soup	44
Pumpkin and Sage Soup	45
Coconut Garlic Mushroom Soup	45
Parmesan Basil Tomato Soup	46
Squash Pear Soup	47
Thai-Inspired Vegetable Noodle Soup	48

Chapter 9
Creamy Soups — 49
Chilled Courgette and Cream Soup	50
Creamy Mushroom and Tofu Soup	50
Cream of Cauliflower Soup	51
Creamy Ham and Potato Soup	51
Creamy Chicken and Sweetcorn Soup	52
Creamy Chicken Soup	52
Creamy Cullen Skink Soup	53
Creamy Spinach and Artichoke Soup	54
Chicken and Spiced Black Bean Soup	54

Chapter 10
Festive Soups — 55
Mexican Chocolate Chili Soup	56
Sichuan Spicy Mapo Tofu Soup	56
Cheesy Taco Soup	57
Czech Christmas Soup	57
Asian Chicken Soup	58
Spiced Root Vegetable Medley Soup	59
Mediterranean Greens and Tomato Soup	59
French Onion and Parmesan Soup	60
Greek Spicy Feta and Olive Soup	60
Spicy Thai Green Curry Soup	61
Roasted Butternut Squash Soup with Sage and Crème Fraîche	61

Appendix 1 Measurement Conversion Chart — 62
Appendix 2 The Dirty Dozen and Clean Fifteen — 63
Appendix 3 Index — 64

Introduction

In the realm of culinary exploration, few kitchen appliances have earned their place as indispensably as the soup maker. It's not merely a gadget; it's a transformative force, a conduit for creativity, and a vessel for nourishment. As we embark on this gastronomic journey through The Complete Soup Maker Cookbook, we step into a world where humble ingredients become exquisite soups, and where the act of cooking transcends the ordinary to become a profound expression of artistry.

Soups, in their myriad forms, have long held a cherished spot in the culinary landscape. They are the embodiment of comfort, warmth, and nourishment, transcending cultural boundaries to grace tables across the globe. Yet, the advent of the soup maker has revolutionized the way we approach soup-making. It's not just about boiling ingredients in water; it's about orchestrating flavors, textures, and aromas with precision, guided by the intuitive hands of a chef armed with a visionary soup maker.

In these pages, you will find a symphony of recipes that celebrate the versatility of the soup maker. From velvety bisques that caress the palate to hearty stews that evoke a sense of satisfaction, each recipe is a testament to the boundless possibilities that unfold when innovation meets tradition. Whether you are a seasoned chef seeking new inspiration or a novice cook eager to explore the realm of soups, this cookbook beckons you into a world where every spoonful is a journey in itself.

Beyond the mere amalgamation of ingredients, this cookbook delves into the art and science of soup making. It unravels the secrets behind coaxing flavors to dance harmoniously, exploring the nuances of spice, the subtleties of herbs, and the alchemy of broth-making. With each turn of the page, you'll discover not just recipes, but a culinary education that empowers you to experiment, create, and savor the fruits of your kitchen labor.

The Complete Soup Maker Cookbook is not merely a collection of recipes; it's a guide that invites you to embark on a gastronomic odyssey. It encourages you to push the boundaries of your culinary prowess, to embrace the joy of experimentation, and to revel in the delightful surprises that emerge when you allow your creativity to flourish. Whether you're preparing a soul-soothing soup for a quiet evening at home or hosting a gathering that demands culinary finesse, this cookbook is your trusted companion, ready to elevate your soup-making endeavors to new heights.

As you leaf through these pages and immerse yourself in the world of soups crafted with a dash of innovation and a dollop of passion, remember that each recipe is an invitation to embark on a culinary adventure. So, don your apron, fire up your soup maker, and let the journey begin—one ladleful at a time.

Chapter 1

Embark on Your Soup-Making Odyssey

The Soup Maker Revolution Unveiled

In the annals of culinary history, the evolution of soup making stands as a testament to humanity's ingenuity in transforming simple ingredients into extraordinary sustenance. This chapter delves into the metamorphosis of soup creation over time and introduces the instrumental force that has propelled it into the 21st century—the soup maker.

THE EVOLUTION OF SOUP MAKING:

To truly understand the soup maker revolution, one must first trace the roots of soup culture. Soup, in its most elemental form, has been a culinary mainstay across diverse cultures and epochs. From the humble pots simmering over ancient hearths to the sophisticated kitchens of today, the journey of soup making is a fascinating exploration of culinary evolution.

In ancient civilizations, soups were born out of necessity, utilizing locally available ingredients to create nourishing, hearty meals. As societies progressed, so did the art of soup making. Recipes became more refined, and regional variations emerged, each reflecting the unique tastes and preferences of its inhabitants.

The advent of technology marked a significant turning point. Traditional methods of slow simmering in large pots gave way to more efficient and time-saving techniques. This shift paved the way for the emergence of the modern soup maker—a device designed to streamline the soup-making process without compromising the integrity of flavors.

THE SIGNIFICANCE OF THE SOUP MAKER:

Why has the soup maker become an indispensable tool in contemporary kitchens? The answer lies in its ability to democratize the art of soup making. No longer confined to the realm of seasoned chefs or elaborate kitchens, soup making has become accessible to the everyday cook, thanks to the convenience and efficiency offered by soup makers.

Soup makers bridge the gap betweeculinary tradition and the fast-paced lifestyles of the modern world. They empower individuals to create wholesome, flavorful soups with minimal effort, allowing for a seamless integration of homemade goodness into busy schedules. From soups that evoke childhood memories to experimental creations that push the boundaries of flavor, the soup maker has become a versatile companion in the kitchen.

This culinary revolution extends beyond practicality—it represents a shift in the way we approach food. The soup maker encourages a return to wholesome, homemade meals, fostering a deeper connection to the ingredients that nourish us. It transforms cooking from a chore into an enjoyable and rewarding experience, where creativity and experimentation are not only welcomed but celebrated.

Tips for Soup Maker Mastery

INGREDIENT PREP:
- Chop ingredients uniformly to ensure even cooking.
- Layer ingredients strategically for optimal blending and flavor infusion.
- Preheat broth or liquids to expedite the cooking process.

FLAVOR LAYERING:
- Add ingredients in stages to build complexity.
- Start with aromatics like onions and garlic, followed by vegetables, proteins, and herbs.
- Experiment with adding certain ingredients towards the end for a burst of freshness.

SPICE SENSIBILITY:
- Exercise caution with potent spices; they can intensify during the cooking process.
- Taste and adjust spice levels gradually to avoid overpowering the soup.

BROTH BRILLIANCE:
- Use homemade broths for unparalleled flavor, or enhance store-bought ones with aromatic elements.
- Experiment with different broth bases to match the profile of your soup.

TEXTURE MATTERS:
- Vary ingredient sizes for diverse textures.
- For creamier soups, blend for a longer duration, or pulse for chunkier varieties.

EXPERIMENTATION IS KEY:
- Don't shy away from unconventional ingredients; soup making is a canvas for creativity.
- Challenge yourself with unique flavor combinations and unexpected elements.

SEASONING SAVVY:
- Season sparingly at the beginning; you can always adjust later.
- Taste as you go, paying attention to the evolving flavor profile.

TEMPERATURE CONTROL:
- Familiarize yourself with your soup maker's temperature settings.
- Adjust cooking times based on the consistency and thickness desired.

FRESH FINISHING TOUCHES:
- Add fresh herbs, a drizzle of quality olive oil, or a splash of citrus just before serving.
- These finishing touches add a burst of vibrancy and elevate the overall dining experience.

CLEANING AND MAINTENANCE:
- Follow the manufacturer's guidelines for cleaning your soup maker.
- Regular maintenance ensures longevity and optimal performance.

The Art and Science of Soup Making

MASTERING FLAVOR PROFILES:

At the heart of every exceptional soup lies the mastery of flavor profiles. The interplay between sweet and savory, the delicate dance of spices, and the elusive essence of umami—these are the brushstrokes that paint the canvas of a well-crafted soup.

Balancing sweet and savory elements is a fundamental aspect of soup making. Whether it's the natural sweetness of root vegetables in a hearty stew or the subtle sweetness of caramelized onions in a French onion soup, understanding and harmonizing these flavors elevate the dining experience.

The pursuit of umami, often referred to as the fifth taste, adds depth and richness to soups. Umami is the savory, meaty flavor that tantalizes the taste buds. Achieving the perfect umami balance involves a careful selection of ingredients, such as mushrooms, soy sauce, or Parmesan cheese, to impart that elusive and satisfying complexity to the soup.

SPICE AND HERB ALCHEMY:

The artful use of spices and herbs is where soup making transcends from mere sustenance to a sensory delight. Each spice and herb contributes its unique personality, transforming a simple broth into a complex and aromatic elixir.

Elevating flavors with spices involves a nuanced understanding of the characteristics of each spice. Whether it's the warmth of cinnamon in a Moroccan lentil soup or the earthiness of cumin in a chili, the judicious use of spices enhances the overall flavor profile without overwhelming the palate.

Fresh herbs, with their vibrant and aromatic qualities, add a layer of freshness to soups. Whether it's the bright notes of basil in a tomato bisque or the earthy undertones of rosemary in a potato leek soup, herbs contribute to the overall balance and fragrance of the dish.

THE ANATOMY OF BROTHS:

At the core of every soup is the foundation of its flavor—the broth. Crafting the perfect broth is a nuanced skill that involves extracting the essence of ingredients while maintaining a delicate balance.

The journey of creating a flawless soup base begins with selecting quality ingredients. Whether it's simmering bones for a rich bone broth or coaxing flavors from vegetables for a hearty vegetable broth, the choice of components influences the character of the soup.

Experimenting with broth varieties opens a realm of possibilities. From classic chicken and beef broths to vegetable and seafood bases, each imparts a unique character to the soup. Understanding the nuances of different broths allows for a tailored approach to recipe creation, expanding the repertoire of flavors at the chef's disposal.

The soup maker revolution is not merely about technological innovation; it is a celebration of the rich tapestry of culinary history interwoven with the threads of modern convenience. As we embark on this journey through The Soup Maker Cookbook, we invite you to savor not just the recipes but the profound transformation of an ancient culinary art into a contemporary expression of creativity and nourishment. The soup maker, in its significance, encapsulates the essence of culinary evolution—a journey that continues to unfold with each simmering pot and every ladleful of homemade goodness.

Chapter 2

Stocks and Broths

Rich Beef Broth

Prep time: 15 minutes | Cook time: 3 hours | Yields: Approximately 2 litres

- 1 kg beef bones (marrow and knuckle)
- 2 carrots, chopped
- 2 celery stalks, chopped
- 1 onion, quartered
- 3 cloves garlic, crushed
- 2 sprigs fresh thyme
- 1 bay leaf
- Salt and pepper to taste

1. Roast beef bones in the oven until browned.
2. Place the roasted bones, carrots, celery, onion, garlic, thyme, bay leaf, salt, and pepper in the soup maker.
3. Fill with enough water to cover the ingredients.
4. Strain the broth and discard solids.
5. Use as a flavorful base for stews and sauces.

Classic Chicken Stock

Prep time: 10 minutes | Cook time: 2 hours | Yields: Approximately 2 litres

- 1 whole chicken carcass
- 2 carrots, chopped
- 2 celery stalks, chopped
- 1 onion, quartered
- 2 cloves garlic, crushed
- Handful of fresh parsley
- 2 bay leaves
- Salt and pepper to taste

1. Place the chicken carcass, carrots, celery, onion, garlic, parsley, bay leaves, salt, and pepper in the soup maker.
2. Fill with enough water to cover the ingredients.
3. Set the soup maker to the "broth" or "soup" setting and let it simmer for about 2 hours.
4. Strain the stock and discard solids.
5. Use as a base for soups or other recipes.

Vegetable Stock

Prep time: 10 minutes | Cook time: 1 hour | Yields: Approximately 1.5 litres

- 2 carrots, chopped
- 2 celery stalks, chopped
- 1 onion, chopped
- 1 leek, sliced
- 2 cloves garlic, crushed
- Handful of fresh parsley
- Salt and pepper to taste

1. Place carrots, celery, onion, leek, garlic, parsley, bay leaf, salt, and pepper in the soup maker.
2. Fill with enough water to cover the ingredients.
3. Set the soup maker to the "broth" or "soup" setting and let it simmer for about 1 hour.
4. Strain the stock and discard solids.
5. Use as a vegetarian base for various dishes.

Mushroom Broth

Prep time: 10 minutes | Cook time: 1 hour | Yields: Approximately 1.5 litres

- 500g assorted mushrooms (shiitake, cremini, button), sliced
- 1 onion, chopped
- 2 cloves garlic, minced
- 1 leek, sliced
- 1 carrot, chopped
- Handful of fresh thyme
- Salt and pepper to taste

1. Sauté mushrooms, onion, garlic, leek, and carrot until softened.
2. Place the sautéed mixture, thyme, bay leaf, salt, and pepper in the soup maker.
3. Set the soup maker to the "broth" or "soup" setting and let it simmer for about 1 hour.
4. Strain the broth and discard solids.
5. Use as a savory base for mushroom-based dishes.

Fish Stock

Prep time: 15 minutes | Cook time: 45 minutes | Yields: Approximately 1.5 litres

- Fish bones and trimmings (from white fish)
- 1 onion, chopped
- 2 carrots, chopped
- 2 celery stalks, chopped
- 1 leek, sliced
- 2 cloves garlic, crushed
- Handful of fresh parsley
- 1 bay leaf
- Salt and pepper to taste

1. Rinse fish bones and trimmings under cold water.
2. Place fish bones, onion, carrots, celery, leek, garlic, parsley, bay leaf, salt, and pepper in the soup maker.
3. Strain the stock and discard solids.
4. Use for seafood soups and risottos.

Turkey Bone Broth

Prep time: 15 minutes | Cook time: 2 hours | Yields: Approximately 2 litres

- 1 turkey carcass
- 2 carrots, chopped
- 2 celery stalks, chopped
- 1 onion, quartered
- 2 cloves garlic, crushed
- Handful of fresh sage
- 1 bay leaf
- Salt and pepper to taste

1. Place the turkey carcass, carrots, celery, onion, garlic, sage, bay leaf, salt, and pepper in the soup maker.
2. Set the soup maker to the "broth" or "soup" setting and let it simmer for about 2 hours.
3. Strain the broth and discard solids.
4. Use for hearty soups and stews.

The Complete Soup Maker Cookbook | 9

Chapter 3

Grain, Beans and Lentils Soup Recipes

Pasta and Bean with Basil Oil Soup

Prep time: 10 minutes | **Cook time:** 15 minutes | Serves 6

- 2 tablespoons extra virgin olive oil
- 1 onion, diced
- 3 garlic cloves, crushed
- 1 tablespoon finely chopped rosemary
- 2 x 400 g (13 oz) cans chopped tomatoes
- 600 ml (1 pint) vegetable stock
- Grated Parmesan cheese, to serve
- For the basil oil (optional)
- 25 g (1 oz) basil leaves
- 150 ml (¼ pint) extra virgin olive oil

1. Heat the oil in the soup maker using the sauté function. Add the onion, garlic and rosemary and sauté for 5 minutes until the onion is softened, stirring frequently with a wooden spatula.
2. Serve the soup in warm bowls, drizzled with a little of the basil oil, if liked, and sprinkled with some Parmesan.

Seasoned White Bean Soup

Prep time: 10 minutes | **Cook time:** 20 minutes | Serves 4

- 1 tbsp olive oil
- 250g/9oz dried cannellini beans, pre soaked
- 1 onion, chopped
- 1 celery stalk, chopped
- 3 garlic cloves, crushed
- 2 ripe tomatoes, chopped
- 1 bay leaf (removed before blending)
- 1 tbsp dried thyme
- 1 tbsp freshly chopped parsley
- 750ml/3 cups vegetable stock
- Salt and pepper to taste

1. Choose your preferred blend function, if required. Otherwise decide on your consistency at the end of cooking and then blend.
2. If your soup maker has a browning function, add the olive oil and onions first and leave to brown for a few minutes.

Spicy Black Bean Soup

Prep time: 10 minutes | Cook time: 10 minutes | Serves 4

- 400g canned black beans, drained and rinsed
- 400g canned diced tomatoes
- 1 onion, chopped
- 2 cloves garlic, minced
- 1 litre vegetable broth
- Salt and pepper to taste

1. Place black beans, diced tomatoes, onion, and garlic in the soup maker.
2. Add vegetable broth and chilli powder.
3. Set the soup maker to the "smooth" setting and let it blend and cook.
4. Season with salt and pepper to taste.
5. Serve hot, garnished with chopped fresh coriander and a dollop of yoghurt (or dairy-free yoghurts).

Broad Bean and Mint Soup

Prep time: 10 minutes | Cook time: 20 minutes | Serves 4

- 550 g (1 lb) frozen broad beans, thawed
- 2 tablespoons olive oil
- 2 shallots, diced
- 1 large carrot, diced
- 1 celery stick, diced
- 900 ml (1½ pints) vegetable stock
- 1 tablespoon chopped mint leaves
- Salt and pepper
- 4 tablespoons double cream, to serve

1. Blanch the broad beans in a saucepan of boiling water for 3–4 minutes, then drain and refresh under cold running water. Peel off the tough outer skins.
2. Season the soup to taste, then pour into warm bowls. Swirl through the cream before serving.

Winter Lentil and Vegetable Soup

Prep time: 10 minutes | Cook time: 40 minutes | Serves 2

- 2 carrots, topped and tailed then sliced lengthways
- 85g dried lentils, preferably red ones
- 3 pieces celery – cut lengthways
- 2 leeks – cut into thin circular pieces
- 2 tbsp tomato puree
- 2 tsp ground coriander
- 1 tsp dried thyme leaves if desired

1. This couldn't be easier! Simply place all the ingredients in your soup making machine.
2. Add 1.5 litres of boiling water and select a lower heat for your soup making machine.
3. Cook for approximately 30 minutes.
4. Serve and enjoy.
5. If you want it thicker you can add a little flour when cooking.

Mexican Lime, Bean and Tomato Soup

Prep time: 10 minutes | Cook time: 30 minutes | Serves 4

- 1 tbsp olive oil
- 2 garlic cloves, crushed
- 1 red chilli, deseeded and chopped
- 1 red onion, chopped
- 2 tbsp lime juice
- 3 tbsp freshly chopped coriander/basil
- Salt and pepper to taste

1. Choose your preferred blend function, if required. Otherwise decide on your consistency at the end of cooking and then blend.
2. Add all the ingredients to the soup maker, except the lime juice. Cover and leave to cook on high for 30 minutes.
3. Ensure all the ingredients are well. Stir through the lime juice, adjust the seasoning and serve.

The Complete Soup Maker Cookbook | 13

Lentil and Tomato Soup

Prep time: 10 minutes | Cook time: 10 minutes | Serves 4

- 200g red lentils
- 500g ripe tomatoes, chopped
- 1 onion, chopped
- 2 cloves garlic, minced
- 1 litre vegetable broth
- 15ml olive oil
- Salt and pepper to taste

1. Sauté onion and garlic in olive oil until softened.
2. Add red lentils, chopped tomatoes, and vegetable broth.
3. Cook until lentils are tender.
4. Blend until smooth.
5. Season with salt and pepper.
6. Serve hot.

Mexican Bean Soup

Prep time: 10 minutes | Cook time: 7 minutes | Serves 4

- 2 tablespoons vegetable oil
- 1 large onion, diced
- 1 red pepper, cored, deseeded and diced
- 2 garlic cloves, finely chopped
- 30 g (1 oz) sachet Mexican fajita, taco or chilli con carne spice mix
- 4 tablespoons soured cream
- 25 g (1 oz) tortilla chips (optional)

1. Heat the oil in the soup maker using the sauté function. Add the garlic and spice mix and cook, stirring, for another 1–2 minutes.
2. Serve the soup in warm bowls, drizzled with the soured cream and topped with the tortilla chips, if liked.

Healthy Chickpea Split Pea Soup

Prep time: 10 minutes | Cook time: 38 minutes | Serves 6

- 225 g dry red split peas, rinsed and soaked for 2 hours
- 0.45 g cayenne powder
- 0.45 g cinnamon
- 0.45 g paprika
- 0.45 g turmeric
- 15 ml fresh lemon juice
- 128 g carrot, diced
- 150 g onion, diced
- 6.9 g sea salt

1. Heat oil in a pan over medium heat. Add carrots, onion, ginger, and garlic and sauté until onion is softened. Transfer to the soup maker.
2. Add remaining ingredients to the soup maker and stir well. Seal soup maker with lid and cook on chunky mode for 28 minutes. Serve and enjoy.

Hearty Lentil and Vegetable Soup

Prep time: 15 minutes | Cook time: 1 hour | Serves: 4-6

- 1 tablespoon olive oil
- 1 onion, chopped
- 2 carrots, diced
- 2 celery stalks, diced
- 2 cloves garlic, minced
- 225g dried green lentils
- 1.6 litres vegetable broth
- 1 teaspoon dried thyme
- 2.5g salt
- 1.25g black pepper

1. Add the olive oil, onion, carrots, celery, and garlic to the soup maker.
2. Stir in the lentils, vegetable broth, thyme, salt, and pepper.
3. Close the lid and set the soup maker to the "soup" setting.
4. Allow the soup to cook for 1 hour, or until the lentils are tender.

Chapter 4

Poultry Soup Recipes

Top Turkey and Wild Rice Soup

Prep time: 10 minutes | Cook time: 10 minutes | Serves 4

- 250g cooked turkey, diced
- 100g wild rice, cooked
- 1 onion, chopped
- 2 carrots, sliced
- 2 celery stalks, chopped
- 2 cloves garlic, minced
- 1 litre chicken broth
- Salt and pepper to taste

1. Place diced cooked turkey, cooked wild rice, chopped onion, sliced carrots, chopped celery, and minced garlic in the soup maker.
2. Season with salt and pepper to taste.
3. Serve hot.

Red Bean Turkey Soup

Prep time: 10 minutes | Cook time: 33 minutes | Serves 4

- 177 g can red beans, rinsed and drained
- 1/2 lb ground turkey, crumbled
- 0.5 g dried oregano
- 5.4 g chili powder
- 1 onion, chopped
- 4 oz can green chilies, diced
- 225 g can tomato, crushed
- 500 ml chicken stock
- Pepper
- Salt

1. Add all ingredients into the soup maker and stir well. Seal soup maker with lid and cook on chunky mode. Season soup with salt and pepper.
2. Serve and enjoy.

The Complete Soup Maker Cookbook

Chicken and Coconut Soup

Prep time: 5 minutes | Cook time: none | Serves 4

- 2 tbsp olive oil
- 1 medium onion, peeled and chopped
- 1 clove garlic, crushed
- 1 tsp ground coriander/basil
- 1 tsp ground cumin
- 750ml/3 cups chicken stock
- 250ml/1 cup coconut milk
- Salt and freshly ground black pepper
- Handful of fresh basil leaves, chopped

1. Choose your preferred blend function, if required. Otherwise decide on your consistency at the end of cooking and then blend.
2. Cook the chicken in advance.
3. If your soup maker has a browning function add the olive oil, onions and garlic first. Leave to brown for a few minutes.
4. Add all the ingredients except the basil to the soup maker. Adjust the seasoning, stir in the basil leaves and serve.

Chicken and Anellini Pasta Soup

Prep time: 10 minutes | Cook time: 45 minutes | Serves 4

- 1 tbsp olive oil
- 1 onion, chopped
- 125g/4oz anellini pasta
- 2 carrots, chopped
- 125g/4oz cauliflower florets
- 750ml/3 cups chicken stock
- 2 tsp dried herbs
- Salt and pepper to taste

1. Choose your preferred blend function, if required. Otherwise decide on your consistency at the end of cooking and then blend.
2. Add all the ingredients to the soup maker. Cover and leave to cook on high for 30 minutes. Ensure all the ingredients are well combined, tender and piping hot. Blend to your preferred consistency Adjust the seasoning and serve.

Garlic Lemon Chicken Soup

Prep time: 5 minutes | Cook time: none | Serves 4

- 250g cooked chicken, shredded
- 200g potatoes, peeled and cubed
- 70g carrot, peeled and chopped
- 3 cloves garlic, crushed
- 100g egg noodles
- 1 tbsp. flour
- 1 litre chicken stock

1. Add all ingredients in your soup maker, breaking the noodles up into small pieces as you put them in. Stir to combine well.
2. Ensure you don't go above the MAX line in your soup maker. If needed, top up to the MIN line with hot water.
3. Put the lid on and select the chunky setting.

Cauliflower Chicken Soup

Prep time: 10 minutes | Cook time: 30 minutes | Serves 4

- 280 g chicken, cooked and shredded
- 170 g cauliflower rice, cooked
- 1.2 g onion powder
- 62.5 ml heavy cream
- 14 oz chicken stock
- 4 oz cream cheese, cubed
- 9.84 g garlic, minced
- 28.4 g butter
- Salt

1. Add all ingredients into the soup maker and stir well. Seal soup maker with lid and cook on chunky mode for 25 minutes.
2. Serve and enjoy.

Jerk Chicken and Sweet Potato Soup

Prep time: 10 minutes | Cook time: 10 minutes | Serves 4

- 2 tablespoons vegetable oil
- 1 red onion, diced
- 1 celery stick, diced
- 2.5 cm (1 inch) piece of fresh root ginger, peeled and diced
- 1 tablespoon jerk seasoning
- 1.2 litres (2 pints) chicken stock
- 2 tablespoons lime juice
- 250 g (8 oz) cooked chicken, shredded
- Salt and pepper
- Thinly sliced spring onions, to garnish

1. Heat the oil in the soup maker using the sauté function. Add the jerk seasoning and the sweet potatoes and cook, stirring, for another minute.
2. Pour into warm bowls and top each with a handful of the shredded chicken. Serve sprinkled with spring onions.

Chicken and Sweetcorn Soup

Prep time: 15 minutes | Cook time: 20 minutes | Serves 6

- 500g chicken breast, shredded
- 150g sweetcorn kernels
- 1 carrot, julienned
- 2 spring onions, chopped
- 1.5 litres chicken broth
- 2 eggs, beaten
- 1 tbsp soy sauce
- Salt and pepper to taste

1. In a soup maker, bring chicken broth to a simmer. Add shredded chicken, sweetcorn, carrot, and spring onions.
2. Cook for about 10 minutes until vegetables are tender.
3. Slowly pour beaten eggs into the soup, stirring continuously.
4. Add soy sauce and season with salt and pepper.
5. Serve hot.

Turkey and Bacon Soup

Prep time: 10 minutes | Cook time: 10 minutes | Serves 4

- 250g cooked turkey, diced
- 200g bacon, chopped
- 1 onion, chopped
- 2 cloves garlic, minced
- 200ml heavy cream
- 1 litre chicken broth
- Salt and pepper to taste

1. In a pan, cook chopped bacon until crispy. Remove and drain on paper towels.
2. Place diced cooked turkey, chopped bacon, chopped onion, minced garlic, and heavy cream in the soup maker.
3. Add chicken broth.
4. Set the soup maker to the "smooth" setting and let it blend and cook.
5. Season with salt and pepper to taste.
6. Serve hot.

Classic Chicken and Asparagus Soup

Prep time: 10 minutes | Cook time: 10 minutes | Serves 4

- 250g chicken breast, diced
- 200g fresh asparagus spears, chopped
- 1 onion, chopped
- 2 cloves garlic, minced
- 200ml heavy cream
- 1 litre chicken broth
- Salt and pepper to taste

1. Place diced chicken breast, chopped fresh asparagus spears, chopped onion, minced garlic, and heavy cream in the soup maker.
2. Add chicken broth.
3. Set the soup maker to the "smooth" setting and let it blend and cook.
4. Season with salt and pepper to taste.
5. Serve hot.

Turkey and Vegetable Quinoa Soup

Prep time: 15 minutes | Cook time: 30 minutes | Serves 6

- 500g turkey, ground
- 200g quinoa, rinsed
- 2 carrots, sliced
- 2 courgette, diced
- 1 onion, chopped
- 2 cloves garlic, minced
- 1.5 litres turkey or chicken broth
- 1 tsp dried oregano
- Salt and pepper to taste

1. In a soup maker, cook ground turkey until browned. Add chopped onions and minced garlic.
2. Stir in quinoa, carrots, courgette, oregano, and broth.
3. Set the soup maker to the desired setting and let it cook for about 20-25 minutes or until quinoa is cooked.
4. Season with salt and pepper to taste.
5. Serve hot.

Sweet Potato and Thai Chicken Soup

Prep time: 10 minutes | Cook time: 45 minutes | Serves 4

- 1 tbsp olive
- 2 garlic cloves, crushed
- ½ tsp each crushed chilli flakes, ground ginger and fish sauce
- 2 tbsp red Thai curry paste
- 1 tsp sugar
- 1 tbsp lime juice
- 75g/3oz watercress
- Salt and pepper to taste

1. Choose your preferred blend function, if required. Otherwise decide on your consistency at the end of cooking and then blend.
2. Add all the ingredients to the soup maker, except the lime juice and watercress. Adjust the seasoning, stir through the lime juice and serve with the watercress piled on top of each soup bowl.

Chicken, Carrot and Corn Soup

Prep time: 10 minutes | Cook time: 10 minutes | Serves: 4-6

- 1 tablespoon olive oil
- 1 onion, chopped
- 1 carrot, diced
- 1 celery stalk, diced
- 2 cloves garlic, minced
- 1 litre chicken broth
- 125ml double cream
- 1.25g salt
- 1.25g black pepper

1. Add the olive oil, onion, carrot, celery, and garlic to the soup maker.
2. Set the soup maker to the "sauté" setting and cook until the vegetables are softened, about 5 minutes.
3. Close the lid and set the soup maker to the "smooth" setting.
4. Allow the soup to cook for 10 minutes.
5. Serve hot.

Hearty Turkey Noodle Soup

Prep time: 15 minutes | Cook time: 10 minutes | Serves: 4-6

- 1 tablespoon olive oil
- 1 onion, chopped
- 2 carrots, diced
- 2 celery stalks, diced
- 2 cloves garlic, minced
- 110g dried egg noodles
- 1 litre turkey broth
- 60ml chopped fresh parsley
- 1.25g salt
- 1.25g black pepper

1. Add the olive oil, onion, carrots, celery, and garlic to the soup maker.
2. Set the soup maker to the "sauté" setting and cook until the vegetables are softened, about 5 minutes.
3. Close the lid and set the soup maker to the "chunky" setting.
4. Allow the soup to cook for 10 minutes.
5. Serve hot.

Chapter 5

Meat Soup Recipes

Beef Stock and Onion Soup

Prep time: 5 minutes | Cook time: none | Serves 4

- 2 large onions, peeled and sliced
- 1 clove garlic, crushed
- 1lt/4 cups beef stock/broth
- 1 tbsp fresh chopped thyme
- 1 tbsp Worcestershire sauce
- Salt and pepper
- 2 tbsp Parmesan cheese, grated
- 2 tbsp Gruyere cheese, grated, to garnish

1. Choose your preferred blend function, if required. Otherwise decide on your consistency at the end of cooking and then blend.
2. If your soup maker has a browning function, add the olive oil and onions first and leave to brown for a few minutes.
3. Add all the ingredients except the Parmesan and Gruyere to the soup maker. Adjust the seasoning and serve topped with a sprinkling of Gruyere.

Pork and Cabbage Stew

Prep time: 15 minutes | Cook time: 1.5 hours | Serves 6

- 500g pork shoulder, cubed
- 1 onion, chopped
- 3 carrots, sliced
- 1/2 small head cabbage, shredded
- 3 potatoes, diced
- 2 cloves garlic, minced
- 1.5 litres pork or vegetable broth
- 1 tsp caraway seeds
- Salt and pepper to taste

1. In a soup maker, brown pork cubes. Add chopped onions and garlic, cook until softened.
2. Stir in carrots, cabbage, potatoes, caraway seeds, and pork broth.
3. Set the soup maker to the desired setting and let it simmer for about 1.5 hours.
4. Season with salt and pepper to taste.
5. Serve warm.

Lamb and Chickpea Soup

Prep time: 15 minutes | Cook time: 40 minutes | Serves 2

- 1 tablespoon olive oil
- 1 sliced onion
- 3 chopped celery sticks
- 2 diced carrots
- 1 teaspoon ground turmeric
- 1 teaspoon cumin
- 1 teaspoon coriander
- 400g tin green lentils
- 210g tin chickpeas
- 2 tbsp tomato puree
- 2 teaspoons vegetable bouillon powder
- ½ small bunch of parsley chopped finely

1. Heat the oil in a large deep pan.
2. Add the diced carrots, sliced onion, and chopped celery along with the pieces of lamb.
3. When its finished cooking your soup, taste it and add salt or pepper if desired.
4. When ready, serve with a sprinkling of chopped parsley on the top.

Italian Spicy Sausage and Pepper Soup

Prep time: 10 minutes | Cook time: 10 minutes | Serves 4

- 250g spicy Italian sausage, sliced
- 1 onion, chopped
- 2 cloves garlic, minced
- 1 red chilli pepper, chopped (adjust to taste)
- 1 litre chicken broth
- 400g diced tomatoes
- 1 red bell pepper, chopped
- 1 yellow bell pepper, chopped
- 1 green bell pepper, chopped
- Fresh basil leaves (for garnish)
- Grated Parmesan cheese (for garnish)

1. Sauté sliced spicy Italian sausage in a soup maker until browned. Remove and set aside.
2. Return the sausage to the pot.
3. Select the "soup" function and let it simmer until flavours meld.
4. Garnish with fresh basil leaves and grated Parmesan cheese.
5. Serve hot.

Hearty Beef and Vegetable Soup

Prep time: 20 minutes | Cook time: 2 hours | Serves 6

- 500g beef stew meat, cubed
- 1 onion, chopped
- 3 carrots, sliced
- 2 potatoes, diced
- 2 celery stalks, chopped
- 3 cloves garlic, minced
- 1.5 litres beef broth
- 1 can (400g) diced tomatoes
- 2 bay leaves
- 1 tsp dried thyme
- Salt and pepper to taste

1. In a soup maker, brown beef cubes. Add chopped onions and garlic, cook until softened.
2. Set the soup maker to the desired setting and let it simmer for about 2 hours.
3. Season with salt and pepper to taste.
4. Serve hot.

Beef and Vegetable Soup

Prep time: 15 minutes | Cook time: 1 hour | Serves 6

- 500g beef stew meat, cubed
- 2 carrots, sliced
- 2 potatoes, diced
- 1 onion, chopped
- 2 cloves garlic, minced
- 1.5 litres beef broth
- 1 bay leaf
- Salt and pepper to taste

1. In a soup maker, brown beef cubes in a bit of oil.
2. Add chopped onions and minced garlic, cook until softened.
3. Pour in beef broth, add carrots, potatoes, and bay leaf.
4. Set the soup maker to the desired setting and let it cook for about 1 hour or until beef is tender.
5. Season with salt and pepper to taste.
6. Serve hot.

Lamb and Barley Soup

Prep time: 20 minutes | Cook time: 1.5 hours | Serves 6

- 500g lamb, diced
- 200g pearl barley
- 2 leeks, sliced
- 3 carrots, diced
- 2 celery stalks, chopped
- 2 litres lamb or vegetable broth
- 1 tsp dried thyme
- Salt and pepper to taste

1. In a soup maker, brown lamb in a pot. Add leeks, carrots, and celery, cook until vegetables are softened.
2. Stir in pearl barley, thyme, and broth.
3. Set the soup maker to the desired setting and let it cook for 1.5 hours or until lamb and barley are tender.
4. Season with salt and pepper to taste.
5. Serve warm.

Pork and Bean Soup

Prep time: 20 minutes | Cook time: 1 hour | Serves 6

- 500g pork shoulder, cubed
- 1 onion, chopped
- 2 cloves garlic, minced
- 400g cannellini beans, drained and rinsed
- 2 carrots, diced
- 1.5 litres pork or vegetable broth
- 1 tsp dried rosemary
- Salt and pepper to taste

1. In a soup maker, brown pork cubes. Add chopped onions and minced garlic.
2. Stir in beans, carrots, rosemary, and broth.
3. Set the soup maker to the desired setting and let it cook for 1 hour or until pork is cooked through.
4. Season with salt and pepper to taste.
5. Serve warm.

Bolognese Beef Soup

Prep time: 5 minutes | Cook time: none | Serves 4

- 1tbsp olive oil
- 200g beef mince, cooked
- 1 onion, chopped
- 3 cloves garlic, crushed
- 2tsp mixed dried herbs
- 400g can chopped tomatoes
- 750ml beef stock
- 50g grated parmesan (optional

1. Add all the ingredients to your soup maker apart from the parmesan.
2. Ensure you don't go over the MAX line on your soup maker. If required, top up to the MIN line with hot water.
3. Set the soup maker to the smooth setting.
4. Once finished, stir in the parmesan cheese until melted (optional).

Venison and Root Vegetable Stew

Prep time: 20 minutes | Cook time: 2 hours | Serves 6

- 500g venison, cubed
- 3 parsnips, peeled and diced
- 3 carrots, peeled and diced
- 2 onions, chopped
- 2 cloves garlic, minced
- 1.5 litres venison or beef broth
- 2 tbsp tomato paste
- 2 tsp dried thyme
- Salt and pepper to taste

1. In a soup maker, brown venison cubes. Add chopped onions and minced garlic.
2. Stir in parsnips, carrots, tomato paste, thyme, and broth.
3. Season with salt and pepper to taste.
4. Serve warm.

The Complete Soup Maker Cookbook | 29

Tomato and Sausage Soup

Prep time: 15 minutes | Cook time: 30 minutes | Serves: 4-6

- 1 tablespoon olive oil
- 1 onion, chopped
- 2 cloves garlic, minced
- 4 cups vegetable broth
- 1/2 teaspoon dried oregano
- 2.5g salt
- 1.25g black pepper
- 125ml double cream

1. Add the olive oil, onion, and garlic to the soup maker.
2. Set the soup maker to the "sauté" setting and cook until the onion is softened, about 5 minutes.
3. Allow the soup to cook for 20 minutes.
4. Using an immersion blender or a regular blender, blend the soup until smooth.
5. Stir in the double cream and heat through.

Chunky Beef Stew

Prep time: 20 minutes | Cook time: 1 hour and 30 minutes | Serves: 4-6

- 1 tablespoon olive oil
- 1 onion, chopped
- 2 carrots, diced
- 2 celery stalks, diced
- 2 cloves garlic, minced
- 4 cups beef broth
- 1 teaspoon dried thyme
- 2.5g salt
- 1.25g black pepper

1. Add the olive oil, onion, carrots, celery, and garlic to the soup maker.
2. Add the beef stew meat and cook until browned on all sides.
3. Stir in the diced tomatoes, beef broth, thyme, salt, and pepper.
4. Allow the stew to cook for 1 hour and 30 minutes, or until the beef is tender.

Chapter 6

Bacon and Ham Soup Recipes

Ham and Potato Soup

Prep time: 20 minutes | Cook time: 40 minutes | Serves 8

- 4 potatoes, peeled then cut into small cubes
- 1 litre chicken stock
- 400g cooked ham, cut into small pieces
- 4 pieces celery finely sliced
- 2 onions, peeled then finely sliced
- 50g unsalted butter
- 100g flour
- 300ml milk – full or semi
- Salt and pepper to taste

1. Start by putting a little of the butter in a frying pan and warming it on the stove.
2. Add the potato cubes and simmer for 5 minutes to soften them.
3. Taste the soup and add salt and pepper if required.
4. Serve immediately, ensuring it is smooth.
5. Add a few sprigs of parsley to the top and a little grated cheese if desired.
6. Serve with fresh bread.

Bacon Squash Soup

Prep time: 5 minutes | Cook time: none | Serves 4

- 2 tbsp olive oil
- 1 medium butternut squash, peeled, de-seeded and chopped
- 1 medium onion, peeled and chopped
- 2 cloves garlic, crushed
- Salt and pepper
- ½ tsp dried thyme
- 1lt/4 cups chicken stock

1. Choose your preferred blend function, if required. Otherwise decide on your consistency at the end of cooking and then blend.
2. If your soup maker has a browning function, add the oil, squash, onions, pepper and leave to brown for ten minutes. If your machine doesn't brown, roast these ingredients in the oven for 30-40 minutes at 180C/350F/Gas4.
3. Add all the ingredients to the soup maker. Adjust the seasoning and serve.

Ham and Pea with Crispy Bacon Soup

Prep time: 10 minutes | Cook time: 113 minutes | Serves 4

- 2 tablespoons olive or vegetable oil
- 1 large onion, diced
- 300 g (10 oz) frozen peas
- 1 litre (1¾ pints) ham or vegetable stock
- 300 g (10 oz) piece of cooked ham, cut into bite-sized pieces
- 8 rindless streaky bacon rashers
- Pepper
- Crusty white bread, to serve

1. Heat the oil in the soup maker using the sauté function. Add the onion, potato and garlic and sauté for 6–7 minutes, stirring frequently with a wooden spatula.
2. Add the peas, stock and ham and season well with pepper. Cook on the Smooth setting.
3. Pour the soup into warm bowls and top with the crispy bacon. Serve with crusty white bread.

Old English Pea and Ham Soup

Prep time: 10 minutes | Cook time: 8 minutes | Serves 4

- 1 tablespoon olive oil
- 2 onions, diced
- 2 celery sticks, diced
- 1 carrot, diced
- 4 tablespoons chopped parsley
- Salt and pepper
- Crusty bread, to serve

1. Heat the oil in in the soup maker using the sauté function. Add the onion, celery and carrot and sauté for 6–8 minutes until softened, stirring frequently with a wooden spatula.
2. Add the peas, stock and mustard, then cook on the Smooth or Chunky setting, whichever you prefer (the soup pictured was prepared using the Chunky setting).
3. Stir the ham and parsley into the soup and season to taste. Serve in warm bowls with crusty bread.

Sweet Potato and Bacon Soup

Prep time: 5 minutes | Cook time: 5 minutes | Serves 4

- 1 tbsp. olive oil
- 1 medium onion, chopped
- 2 garlic cloves, crushed
- 520g sweet potatoes (approx.4 potatoes), peeled and chopped
- 100g bacon lardons
- 1 tsp. dried basil
- 1 tsp. ground cumin
- 2 tsp. smoked paprika
- 900ml vegetable stock

1. Heat the olive oil in your soup maker if it has a sauté function, if not, heat it in a saucepan.
2. Add the onion, garlic and chopped bacon and sauté for about 4-5 minutes.
3. Ensure you don't go above the MAX line in your soup maker. If needed, top up to the MIN line with hot water. Put the lid on and select the smooth setting.

Smoky Ham and Lentil Soup

Prep time: 15 minutes | Cook time: 30 minutes | Serves 4

- 250g smoked ham, diced
- 200g red lentils
- 1 onion, finely chopped
- 2 carrots, diced
- 2 celery stalks, chopped
- 1.5 litres chicken or vegetable broth
- 2 tsp smoked paprika
- Salt and pepper to taste

1. In a large pot, sauté diced ham until lightly browned.
2. Add chopped onion, carrots, and celery. Cook until vegetables are softened.
3. Stir in red lentils, smoked paprika, and broth.
4. Set the soup maker to the desired setting and let it blend to the desired consistency.
5. Season with salt and pepper to taste.
6. Serve warm.

Beer Cheese and Bacon Soup

Prep time: 15 minutes | Cook time: 40 minutes | Serves 6

- 400g bacon, cut into small pieces
- 1 onion, peeled and diced
- 100g flour
- 100g butter
- 800ml chicken stock
- 250ml cream
- 600g cheddar cheese, grated

1. Start by using a drop of oil in a frying pan to cook the bacon pieces, it should take 5-7 minutes to get them crispy.
2. Remove the bacon from the pan and place it on some kitchen towel to absorb excess grease.
3. Pour your beer into the soup maker slowly, mixing as you do so.
4. Ladle into the bowls and serve with a garnish of chives.

Easy Ham and Broccoli Soup

Prep time: 10 minutes | Cook time: 30 minutes | Serves 3

- 284 g broccoli, chopped
- 134 g, ham, cooked, diced
- 625 ml chicken stock
- 1 small shallot, minced
- 1.64 g garlic, minced
- 14.2 g butter
- Pepper
- Salt

1. Melt butter in a pan over medium heat. Add shallot and garlic sauté until shallot is softened. Transfer to the soup maker.
2. Add remaining ingredients to the soup maker and stir well. Seal soup maker with lid and cook on smooth mode for 15 minutes.
3. Season soup with salt and pepper. Serve and enjoy.

Chapter 7

Fish and Seafood Soup Recipes

Curried Cod Cauliflower Soup

Prep time: 10 minutes | Cook time: 15 minutes | Serves 2

- ½ pound fried cod, diced
- 1/2 lb cauliflower florets
- 3.2 g curry powder
- 1.64 g garlic clove, minced
- 1/2 onion, minced
- 312.5 ml water
- Pepper
- Salt

1. Add all ingredients into the soup maker and stir well. Seal soup maker with lid and cook on chunky mode for 15 minutes.
2. Season soup with salt and pepper. Serve and enjoy.

Coconut Milk and Fresh Crab Soup

Prep time: 10 minutes | Cook time: 30 minutes | Serves 4

- 1 tbsp olive oil
- 500ml/2 cups fish or vegetable stock
- 1 onion, chopped
- 2 tbsp fish sauce
- Salt and pepper to taste

1. Choose your preferred blend function, if required. Otherwise decide on your consistency at the end of cooking and then blend.
2. Add all the ingredients to the soup maker, except the spring onions and chopped coriander. Adjust the seasoning and serve garnished with the chopped coriander and spring onions.

The Complete Soup Maker Cookbook

Spiced Prawn Vermicelli Soup

Prep time: 10 minutes | Cook time: 20 minutes | Serves 4

- 125g/4oz vermicelli noodles
- 750ml/3 cups fish or chicken stock
- 2 tbsp coconut cream
- 2 tbsp fish sauce
- ½ tsp cayenne pepper
- 1 tsp shrimp paste
- 2 tsp freshly grated ginger
- 1 fresh lemon grass stalk, peeled and finely chopped
- Salt and pepper to taste

1. Add all the ingredients to the soup maker, except the coconut cream. Cover and leave to cook on high for 20 minutes.
2. Ensure all the ingredients are well combined, tender and piping hot. Stir in the coconut cream and warm through for a minute or two. Adjust the seasoning and serve.

Thai Fish Curry

Prep time: 5 minutes | Cook time: none | Serves 4

- 400g cod, skinless and boneless, cut into chunks
- 1 inch fresh ginger, peeled and grated (or ½ tsp ground ginger)
- 2tbsp Thai green curry paste
- 1tbsp Thai fish sauce
- 2 Kaffir lime leaves
- Juice of half a lime
- 400ml coconut milk (light)
- 350ml vegetable stock
- Coriander leaves (optional for garnish)

1. Add all the ingredients, except the coriander, to your soup maker.
2. Ensure you don't go over the MAX line of your soup maker. If you need to, top up to the MIN line with hot boiling water, or more coconut milk.
3. Set to the chunky setting on your soup maker.
4. Once complete, garnish with coriander (optional).

Creamy Monkfish and Carrot Soup

Prep time: 5 minutes | Cook time: none | Serves 4

- 50g/2oz butter
- 1 medium onion, peeled and chopped
- 2 medium potatoes, peeled and chopped
- 2 medium carrots, peeled and chopped
- 750ml/3 cups chicken stock/broth
- 120ml/½ cup dry white wine
- 1 tsp dried thyme
- Salt and pepper
- 550g/1¼lb cooked monkfish, skinned and cut into strips
- 120ml/½ cup double cream
- 1 tbsp chopped flat leaf parsley to garnish

1. Choose your preferred blend function, if required. Otherwise decide on your consistency at the end of cooking and then blend.
2. Cook the monkfish in advance.
3. Add all the ingredients except the cream and parsley to the soup maker. and serve garnished with chopped parsley.

Haddock and Sweetcorn Soup

Prep time: 10 minutes | Cook time: 30 minutes | Serves 4

- 3 chopped medium potatoes
- 600ml full-fat milk
- 500ml fish stock
- 400g skinless smoked haddock fillet – cut into pieces
- 200g broccoli
- 2 x 198g tins of sweetcorn
- 2 sliced spring onions
- lemon juice

1. Warm a little oil on the stove.
2. Make sure the potatoes have been cut into small pieces before tipping them into the frying pan.
3. Sauté for 3-5 minutes to soften.
4. Transfer the potatoes to the soup making machine.
5. Pour in the milk and fish stock.
6. Add salt and pepper if required.
7. Serve with a scattering of spring onions.

Smoked Salmon Cabbage Soup

Prep time: 10 minutes | Cook time: 30 minutes | Serves 4

- 1/4 cabbage, sliced
- 2 vegetable stock cubes
- 1 L water
- 340 g potatoes, peeled and diced
- 1.12 g dried rosemary
- 1 garlic clove, minced
- 1 celery stick, sliced
- 1 carrot, diced
- 1 onion, diced
- 15 ml olive oil
- Pepper
- Salt

1. Heat oil in a pan over medium heat. Add onion to the pan and sauté until softened.
2. Add garlic and sauté for 30 seconds. Transfer sautéed onion and garlic to the soup maker.
3. Add smoked salmon and stir well. Season soup with salt and pepper. Serve and enjoy.

Salmon and Dill Soup

Prep time: 5 minutes | Cook time: 3 minutes | Serves 4

- 1tbsp olive oil
- 1 onion, chopped
- 400g can of chopped tomatoes
- 418g can of boneless red salmon, drained and flaked
- 1tbsp fresh lemon juice
- 2tbsps fresh dill, chopped
- 150ml single cream
- 850ml fish stock

1. Heat the olive oil in your soup maker or saucepan.
2. Add the chopped onion and sauté for 2 to 3 minutes.
3. Transfer the ingredients to your soup maker/switch off the sauté function on your soup maker.
4. Put the lid on and select the smooth setting.
5. When the soup has finished add the chopped dill and the single cream. Stir in.

Garlic Mussels and Plum Tomato Soup

Prep time: 10 minutes | Cook time: 40 minutes | Serves 4

- 1 tbsp olive oil
- 5 garlic cloves, crushed
- 4 sweet shallots, chopped
- 200g/7oz fresh plum tomatoes
- 1 tbsp tomato puree/paste
- 500ml/2 cups fish or vegetable stock
- 120ml/ ½ cup dry white wine
- Salt and pepper to taste

1. Choose your preferred blend function, if required. Otherwise decide on your consistency at the end of cooking and then blend.
2. Add all the ingredients to the soup maker. Cover and leave to cook on high for 40 minutes. Ensure all the ingredients are well combined, tender and piping hot. Blend to your preferred consistency Adjust the seasoning and serve.

Thai Fish and Pak Choi Soup

Prep time: 10 minutes | Cook time: 30 minutes | Serves 4

- 125g/4oz egg noodles
- 750ml/3 cups chicken or fish stock
- 2 tbsp Thai red curry paste
- 2 tbsp fish sauce
- 1 tbsp sweet chilli sauce
- 125g/4oz cooked peeled prawns
- 1 Pak Choi, chopped
- 2 tbsp freshly chopped coriander/basil

1. Ensure your soup maker is suitable for cooking with raw fish. If not you should precook it.
2. Choose your preferred blend function, if required. Otherwise decide on your consistency at the end of cooking and then blend.
3. Add all the ingredients to the soup maker, except the chopped coriander. Adjust the seasoning and serve with the chopped coriander sprinkled over the top.

The Complete Soup Maker Cookbook

Clam Chowder Soup

Prep time: 15 minutes | Cook time: 45 minutes | Serves 6

- 2kg clams
- 500g peeled and cubed potatoes
- 300g cubed parsnips
- ½ tablespoon olive oil
- 100g unsmoked bacon lardons
- 1 chopped onion
- 100g crème fraîche

1. Add 1 litre of water to a large pan on a high heat.
2. Once it is boiling, add the clams.
3. Cover and cook for three minutes.
4. Pour into a sieve over a large jug (to keep the cooking water).
5. Throw away any clams which have not opened.
6. Serve topped with the crispy lardons.
7. You can add salt and pepper if desired.

Hearty Salmon and Vegetable Soup

Prep time: 15 minutes | Cook time: 30 minutes | Serves: 4-6

- 1 tablespoon olive oil
- 1 onion, chopped
- 2 carrots, diced
- 2 celery stalks, diced
- 4 cups fish broth
- 1 teaspoon dried dill
- 2.5g salt
- 1.25g black pepper

1. Add the olive oil, onion, carrots, celery, and garlic to the soup maker.
2. Stir in the fish broth, salmon, diced tomatoes, dill, salt, and pepper.
3. Close the lid and set the soup maker to the "soup" setting.
4. Allow the soup to cook for 20 minutes, or until the salmon is cooked through.

Chapter 8

Vegetable Soup Recipes

Spring Greens and Asparagus Soup

Prep time: 10 minutes | Cook time: 10 minutes | Serves 4

- 100g spinach
- 100g watercress
- 100g arugula
- 100g asparagus, chopped
- 1 leek, chopped
- 2 cloves garlic, minced
- 1 litre vegetable broth
- Fresh basil leaves (for garnish)

1. Place spinach, watercress, arugula, chopped asparagus, chopped leek, and minced garlic in the soup maker.
2. Add vegetable broth and let it simmer until the greens are tender.
3. Serve hot, garnished with fresh basil leaves.

Spicy Sweet Potato and Peanut Soup

Prep time: 10 minutes | Cook time: 10 minutes | Serves 4

- 500g sweet potatoes, peeled and diced
- 1 onion, chopped
- 2 cloves garlic, minced
- 2 tbsp peanut butter
- 1 tsp curry powder
- 1 litre vegetable broth
- Salt and pepper to taste

1. Place sweet potatoes, onion, garlic, ginger, peanut butter, and curry powder in the soup maker.
2. Add vegetable broth.
3. Set the soup maker to the "smooth" setting and let it blend and cook.
4. Season with salt and pepper to taste.
5. Serve hot.

Pumpkin and Sage Soup

Prep time: 10 minutes | Cook time: 10 minutes | Serves 4

- 400g pumpkin, peeled and diced
- 1 onion, chopped
- 2 cloves garlic, minced
- 10g fresh sage leaves
- 1 litre vegetable broth
- 15ml olive oil
- Salt and pepper to taste

1. Sauté onion and garlic in olive oil until softened.
2. Add diced pumpkin, fresh sage leaves, and vegetable broth.
3. Cook until pumpkin is tender.
4. Blend until smooth.
5. Season with salt and pepper.
6. Serve hot.

Coconut Garlic Mushroom Soup

Prep time: 10 minutes | Cook time: 30 minutes | Serves 5

- 200g mushrooms, sliced
- 250 ml coconut milk
- 250 ml heavy cream
- 15 ml olive oil
- 500 ml vegetable broth
- 1/2 onion, diced
- Pepper
- Salt

1. Heat oil in a pan over medium heat. Transfer to the soup maker.
2. Add remaining ingredients to the soup maker and stir well. Seal soup maker with lid and cook on smooth mode for 21 minutes. Serve and enjoy.

Bean and Vegan Pesto Soup

Prep time: 15 minutes | Cook time: 45 minutes | Serves 4

- 1 onion, peeled and finely chopped
- 1 courgette – cut into small pieces
- 2 carrots – also cut into small pieces
- 2 tbsp olive oil or the oil of your choice
- 2 cloves of garlic – crushed
- 400g tin of French beans
- 1 litre vegetable stock
- 1 small jar of pesto

1. It should be noted that you can make your own pesto but it is simpler to purchase a jar, just make sure it's vegan-friendly.
2. Place the oil in a saucepan and heat on the hob.
3. Transfer the vegetables to your soup making machine.
4. Give it a quick stir then stir in your jar of pesto.
5. Serve immediately with a drizzle of oil on the top and a little basil.

Parmesan Basil Tomato Soup

Prep time: 10 minutes | Cook time: 30 minutes | Serves 4

- 400 g can tomato, diced
- 2.51 g fresh basil, chopped
- 45g parmesan cheese
- 120 dl heavy cream
- 475 ml chicken stock
- 15 g flour
- 0.51 g dried oregano
- 1.64 g garlic, minced
- 45 g carrot, diced
- Pepper
- Salt

1. Melt the butter in a pan over medium heat. Add onion and sauté for 2 minutes. Sauté the added garlic and cook for 30 seconds.
2. Seal soup maker with lid and cook on smooth mode for 21 minutes. Season soup with salt and pepper. Serve and enjoy.

Squash Pear Soup

Prep time: 10 minutes | Cook time: 30 minutes | Serves 4

- 15 ml vinegar
- 712 ml vegetable stock
- 1.05 g dried sage
- 2 pears, peeled and chopped
- 2 celery, peeled and chopped
- 2 carrots, peeled and chopped
- 3.3 g garlic, minced
- 1 onion, chopped
- 30 ml olive oil
- Pepper
- Salt

1. Heat oil in a pan over medium heat. Add onion and garlic and sauté for 2-3 minutes. Transfer to the soup maker.
2. Add remaining ingredients to the soup maker and stir well. Seal soup maker with lid and cook on smooth mode for 21 minutes.
3. Season soup with salt and pepper. Serve and enjoy.

Lime Sweet Corn Soup

Prep time: 10 minutes | Cook time: 38 minutes | Serves 6

- 815 g fresh sweet corn
- 2 limes, juiced
- 3.2 g parsley
- 9 50 ml chicken stock
- 1 garlic, minced
- 1 small onion, chopped
- 1 small carrot, chopped
- 1 small potato, chopped
- 15 ml olive oil
- Pepper
- Salt

1. Heat oil in a pan over medium heat. Add onion and garlic and sauté for 2-3 minutes. Transfer to the soup maker.
2. Add remaining ingredients to the soup maker and cook on chunky mode for 28 minutes.
3. Season soup with salt and pepper. Serve and enjoy.

Mixed Greens and Fennel Soup

Prep time: 10 minutes | Cook time: 10 minutes | Serves 4

- 100g spinach
- 100g kale
- 100g fennel bulb, sliced
- 100g dandelion greens (or other wild greens)
- 1 onion, chopped
- 2 cloves garlic, minced
- 1 litre vegetable broth
- Fresh tarragon leaves (for garnish)

1. Place spinach, kale, sliced fennel, dandelion greens, chopped onion, and minced garlic in the soup maker.
2. Add vegetable broth and let it simmer until the greens and fennel are tender.
3. Serve hot, garnished with fresh tarragon leaves.

Thai-Inspired Vegetable Noodle Soup

Prep time: 10 minutes | Cook time: 10 minutes | Serves 4

- 200g rice noodles, cooked
- 1 carrot, sliced
- 1 red bell pepper, sliced
- 1 courgette, sliced
- 2 cloves garlic, minced
- 400ml coconut milk
- 1 litre vegetable broth
- 1 tsp red curry paste
- Salt and pepper to taste

1. Place cooked rice noodles, carrot, red bell pepper, courgette, ginger, garlic, and red curry paste in the soup maker.
2. Add coconut milk and vegetable broth.
3. Season with salt and pepper to taste.
4. Serve hot.

Chapter 9

Creamy Soups

Chilled Courgette and Cream Soup

Prep time: 10 minutes | Cook time: 30 minutes | Serves 4

- 1 tbsp olive oil
- 2 onions, chopped
- 450g/1lb courgettes/courgette, chopped
- 500ml/2 cups vegetable stock
- 2 tbsp freshly chopped mint
- 250ml/1 cup single cream
- Salt and pepper to taste

1. Choose your preferred blend function, if required. Otherwise decide on your consistency at the end of cooking and then blend.
2. If your soup maker has a browning function, add the olive oil and onions first and leave to brown for a few minutes.

Creamy Mushroom and Tofu Soup

Prep time: 10 minutes | Cook time: 10 minutes | Serves 4

- 250g mushrooms, sliced
- 200g tofu, cubed
- 1 onion, chopped
- 2 cloves garlic, minced
- 1 litre vegetable broth
- 200ml coconut milk
- Salt and pepper to taste

1. Place mushrooms, tofu, onion, and garlic in the soup maker.
2. Add vegetable broth and coconut milk.
3. Set the soup maker to the "smooth" setting and let it blend and cook.
4. Season with salt and pepper to taste.
5. Serve hot.

Cream of Cauliflower Soup

Prep time: 20 minutes | Cook time: 40 minutes | Serves 6

- 2 tbsp olive oil
- 1 cauliflower cut into small pieces
- 1 onion, peeled and finely sliced
- 3 cloves of garlic crushed
- 200g butter
- 250g flour
- 300ml milk – semi or full-fat will do
- 100ml whipping cream
- 600ml chicken stock
- 100g parmesan cheese - grated
- 3 tbsp ground parsley

1. Place the olive oil in a frying pan and warm it on the stove.
2. Once the oil is hot, add your garlic, cauliflower, and onion.
3. Add the parmesan as you serve, you can also add a drizzle of olive oil.

Creamy Ham and Potato Soup

Prep time: 10 minutes | Cook time: 10 minutes | Serves 4

- 250g cooked ham, diced
- 500g potatoes, peeled and diced
- 1 onion, chopped
- 2 cloves garlic, minced
- 200ml heavy cream
- 1 litre chicken broth
- Salt and pepper to taste

1. Place diced cooked ham, diced potatoes, chopped onion, minced garlic, and heavy cream in the soup maker.
2. Add chicken broth.
3. Set the soup maker to the "smooth" setting and let it blend and cook.
4. Season with salt and pepper to taste.
5. Serve hot.

Creamy Chicken and Sweetcorn Soup

Prep time: 25 minutes | Cook time: 50 minutes | Serves 4

- 1 celery stick
- 1 sliced leek
- 300ml chicken stock
- 250g sweetcorn (crush half lightly with a fork)
- 1 skinless chicken breast cut into cubes
- ½ chopped onion

1. Heat 1 tablespoon of oil in a pan, and add the chicken until it starts to soften. It should only take 5-8 minutes.
2. After 3 minutes add the onion to the pan and sauté with the chicken.
3. Now put the chicken and onion in your soup maker.
4. Taste the soup and add salt and pepper if necessary.
5. Sprinkle with finely chopped chives when you serve.

Creamy Chicken Soup

Prep time: 5 minutes | Cook time: none | Serves 4

- 200g cooked chicken, shredded
- 2 cloves garlic, crushed
- 1 medium onion, chopped
- 200g potatoes scrubbed and diced
- 1litre chicken stock
- 2tbsp crème fraiche

1. Add all the ingredients, except the crème fraiche, to your soup maker and stir to combine.
2. Ensure you don't go above the MAX line in your soup maker. If needed, top up to the MIN line with hot water.
3. Put the lid on and select the smooth setting.
4. Stir in the crème fraiche and manually blend for 15 to 20 seconds.
5. Want to make it less creamy?
6. Just leave out the cream and potatoes (you might need to increase the stock volume).

52 | The Complete Soup Maker Cookbook

Creamy Cullen Skink Soup

Prep time: 10 minutes | Cook time: 32 minutes | Serves 4

- 450 g. haddock, smoked fillets, diced
- 600 ml milk
- 2 celery stalks, sliced
- 1 bay leaf
- 1 onion, diced
- Pepper
- Salt
- Parsley (a handful, for garnish)

1. Transfer all your ingredients, except the bay leaf to the soup maker and stir well.
2. Seal soup maker with lid and cook on smooth mode.
3. Discard bay leaf. Season soup with salt and pepper. Serve and enjoy.

Creamy Broccoli and Almond Soup

Prep time: 10 minutes | Cook time: 10 minutes | Serves 4

- 500g broccoli florets
- 1 onion, chopped
- 2 cloves garlic, minced
- 100g almonds, soaked and peeled
- 1 litre vegetable broth
- Salt and pepper to taste

1. Place broccoli florets, onion, garlic, and soaked almonds in the soup maker.
2. Add vegetable broth.
3. Set the soup maker to the "smooth" setting and let it blend and cook.
4. Season with salt and pepper to taste.
5. Serve hot.

Creamy Spinach and Artichoke Soup

Prep time: 10 minutes | Cook time: 10 minutes | Serves 4

- 200g fresh spinach
- 200g canned artichoke hearts, drained and chopped
- 1 onion, chopped
- 2 cloves garlic, minced
- 200ml coconut milk
- 1 litre vegetable broth
- Salt and pepper to taste

1. Place fresh spinach, chopped artichoke hearts, onion, and garlic in the soup maker.
2. Add coconut milk and vegetable broth.
3. Set the soup maker to the "smooth" setting and let it blend and cook.
4. Season with salt and pepper to taste.
5. Serve hot.

Chicken and Spiced Black Bean Soup

Prep time: 10 minutes | Cook time: 15 minutes | Serves 4

- 2 crushed garlic cloves
- 2 tbsp olive oil
- Finely chopped coriander stalks
- Zest 1 lime and cut into wedges
- 2 teaspoons cumin
- 1 teaspoon chilli flakes
- 400g tin chopped tomatoes
- 400g tin black beans (rinsed and drained)
- 600ml chicken stock
- Flour and corn tortillas – toasted to serve

1. Heat the oil in a large pan.
2. Add the crushed garlic and coriander stalks, then sauté for two minutes.
3. Taste the soup and season if necessary.
4. Serve and sprinkle a little feta, or your preferred cheese on top.

Chapter 10

Festive Soups

Mexican Chocolate Chili Soup

Prep time: 10 minutes | Cook time: 10 minutes | Serves 4

- 400g black beans, cooked and drained
- 30g unsweetened cocoa powder
- 1 red chilli pepper, chopped (adjust to taste)
- 1 litre vegetable broth
- Sour cream (for garnish)
- Chopped coriander (for garnish)

1. Place cooked black beans and chopped red chilli pepper in the soup maker.
2. Add vegetable broth and let it simmer until the beans are heated through.
3. Stir in unsweetened cocoa powder.
4. Serve hot, garnished with a dollop of sour cream and chopped coriander.

Sichuan Spicy Mapo Tofu Soup

Prep time: 10 minutes | Cook time: 10 minutes | Serves 4

- 200g tofu, cubed
- 250g ground pork
- 2 cloves garlic, minced
- 1-inch piece ginger, minced
- Cooked white rice (for serving)

1. Sauté ground pork in a soup maker until browned. Remove and set aside.
2. In the same pot, sauté minced garlic, pepper until fragrant.
3. Return the pork to the pot.
4. Stir in soy sauce, Sichuan peppercorn oil, and doubanjiang.
5. Serve hot with sliced green onions and cooked white rice.

Cheesy Taco Soup

Prep time: 10 minutes | Cook time: 40 minutes | Serves 4

- 2 tbsp olive oil
- 400g ground beef
- 1 tin (400g) chopped tomatoes
- 400ml beef stock
- 200g cream cheese
- 100ml cream

1. Put the olive oil in a pan and warm it on the stove.
2. Add the ground beef and simmer for 3-5 minutes. The aim is to eliminate the pinkness of the meat.
3. Set up the soup making machine and add the ground beef.
4. When ready check and add salt and pepper, if required.
5. Serve with your choice of garnish and accompaniment.

Czech Christmas Soup

Prep time: 30 minutes | Cook time: 60 minutes | Serves 6

- 400g fresh peas – defrosted frozen ones will do
- 1 carrot, topped and tailed then cut into chunks
- 2 pieces of celery cut into large chunks
- 3 cloves of garlic, peeled and crushed
- 1 litre vegetable stock
- Herbs as desired

1. Fresh or tinned peas are best as they won't damage the blades in your soup maker. If you're using frozen peas let them defrost in a pan of warm water before you start.
2. Add the peas, celery, carrot, onion, and garlic to your soup maker.
3. Mix then add the vegetable stock.
4. Serve with your choice of garnish.

Asian Chicken Soup

Prep time: 10 minutes | Cook time: 26 minutes | Serves 4

- 2 chicken breasts, cooked and diced
- 1 L chicken stock
- 52 g spring onions, sliced
- 10.54 g ginger, grated
- 1 1/2 red chili, sliced
- 1 dried lemongrass
- 15 ml lemon juice
- 48 g Thai curry paste

1. Add all ingredients into the soup maker and stir well. Seal soup maker with lid and cook on smooth mode for 21 minutes.
2. Stir well and serve.

Korean Kimchi Pancake Soup

Prep time: 10 minutes | Cook time: 10 minutes | Serves 4

- 1 green onion, thinly sliced
- 1 litre vegetable broth
- Sesame seeds (for garnish)
- Gochugaru (Korean red pepper flakes, for garnish)

1. Place sliced kimchi pancakes and thinly sliced green onion in the soup maker.
2. Add vegetable broth and let it simmer until the pancakes are heated through.
3. Serve hot, garnished with sesame seeds and a sprinkle of gochugaru for extra heat.

Spiced Root Vegetable Medley Soup

Prep time: 5 minutes | Cook time: 7 minutes | Serves 4

- 1 tbsp. olive oil
- 1 onion, chopped
- 2 cloves garlic, crushed
- 300g carrots, peeled and chopped
- 150g parsnips, peeled and chopped
- 400g swede, peeled and chopped
- 2tsp garam masala
- 750ml vegetable stock

1. Heat the oil in your soup maker if it has a sauté function. Alternatively heat the oil in a saucepan.
2. Add the chopped onions and sauté for 5 minutes. Add the garlic and garam masala and sauté for a further 2 minutes.
3. Put the lid on and select the smooth setting.

Mediterranean Greens and Tomato Soup

Prep time: 10 minutes | Cook time: 10 minutes | Serves 4

- 100g spinach
- 100g Swiss chard
- 100g collard greens
- 250ml cherry tomatoes, halved
- 1 onion, chopped
- 2 cloves garlic, minced
- 1 litre vegetable broth
- Fresh basil leaves (for garnish)

1. Place spinach, Swiss chard, collard greens, halved cherry tomatoes, chopped onion, and minced garlic in the soup maker.
2. Add vegetable broth and let it simmer until the greens and tomatoes are tender.
3. Serve hot, garnished with fresh basil leaves.

French Onion and Parmesan Soup

Prep time: 5 minutes | Cook time: 8 minutes | Serves 4

- 2tbsp olive oil
- 500g onions, chopped
- 1 tbsp flour
- 900ml vegetable stock
- 30g parmesan cheese, grated

1. Heat the oil in your soup maker if it has a sauté function. Alternatively, heat the oil in a saucepan.
2. Put the lid on and select the chunky setting.
3. Remove the lid and add the parmesan, stir in until melted.

Greek Spicy Feta and Olive Soup

Prep time: 10 minutes | Cook time: 10 minutes | Serves 4

- 100g feta cheese, crumbled
- 50g Kalamata olives, pitted and sliced
- 1 red chilli pepper, chopped (adjust to taste)
- 1 litre vegetable broth
- Chopped fresh oregano leaves (for garnish)

1. Place crumbled feta cheese, sliced Kalamata olives, and chopped red chilli pepper in the soup maker.
2. Add vegetable broth and let it simmer until the feta cheese is melted.
3. Serve hot, garnished with chopped fresh oregano leaves.

Spicy Thai Green Curry Soup

Prep time: 10 minutes | Cook time: 10 minutes | Serves 4

- 250g chicken breast, sliced
- 400ml coconut milk
- 2 tbsps Thai green curry paste
- 1 litre chicken broth
- 100g bamboo shoots, sliced
- 100g baby corn, sliced
- 50g green beans, chopped
- 1 red chilli pepper, sliced (adjust to taste)
- Fresh basil leaves (for garnish)
- Lime wedges

1. Place sliced chicken breast, coconut milk, Thai green curry paste, and chicken broth in the soup maker.
2. Add bamboo shoots, baby corn, green beans, and red chilli pepper.
3. Garnish with fresh basil leaves and serve with lime wedges.
4. Serve hot.

Roasted Butternut Squash Soup with Sage and Crème Fraîche

Prep time: 10 minutes | Cook time: 45 minutes | Serves 4

- 1 medium butternut squash, peeled and diced
- 1 tablespoon olive oil
- 1 onion, chopped
- 1 teaspoon dried sage
- 1/2 teaspoon salt
- 1/4 teaspoon black pepper
- 4 cups vegetable broth
- 1/2 cup crème fraîche

1. Add the butternut squash and olive oil to the soup maker.
2. Stir in the onion, garlic, sage, salt, and pepper.
3. Set the soup maker to the "soup" setting and cook for 15 minutes.
4. Using an immersion blender or a regular blender, blend the soup until smooth.

Appendix 1 Measurement Conversion Chart

Volume Equivalents (Dry)	
US STANDARD	METRIC (APPROXIMATE)
1/8 teaspoon	0.5 mL
1/4 teaspoon	1 mL
1/2 teaspoon	2 mL
3/4 teaspoon	4 mL
1 teaspoon	5 mL
1 tablespoon	15 mL
1/4 cup	59 mL
1/2 cup	118 mL
3/4 cup	177 mL
1 cup	235 mL
2 cups	475 mL
3 cups	700 mL
4 cups	1 L

Volume Equivalents (Liquid)		
US STANDARD	US STANDARD (OUNCES)	METRIC (APPROXIMATE)
2 tablespoons	1 fl.oz.	30 mL
1/4 cup	2 fl.oz.	60 mL
1/2 cup	4 fl.oz.	120 mL
1 cup	8 fl.oz.	240 mL
1 1/2 cup	12 fl.oz.	355 mL
2 cups or 1 pint	16 fl.oz.	475 mL
4 cups or 1 quart	32 fl.oz.	1 L
1 gallon	128 fl.oz.	4 L

Temperatures Equivalents	
FAHRENHEIT(F)	CELSIUS(C) APPROXIMATE
225 °F	107 °C
250 °F	120 ° °C
275 °F	135 °C
300 °F	150 °C
325 °F	160 °C
350 °F	180 °C
375 °F	190 °C
400 °F	205 °C
425 °F	220 °C
450 °F	235 °C
475 °F	245 °C
500 °F	260 °C

Weight Equivalents	
US STANDARD	METRIC (APPROXIMATE)
1 ounce	28 g
2 ounces	57 g
5 ounces	142 g
10 ounces	284 g
15 ounces	425 g
16 ounces (1 pound)	455 g
1.5 pounds	680 g
2 pounds	907 g

Appendix 2 The Dirty Dozen and Clean Fifteen

The Environmental Working Group (EWG) is a nonprofit, nonpartisan organization dedicated to protecting human health and the environment Its mission is to empower people to live healthier lives in a healthier environment. This organization publishes an annual list of the twelve kinds of produce, in sequence, that have the highest amount of pesticide residue-the Dirty Dozen-as well as a list of the fifteen kinds ofproduce that have the least amount of pesticide residue-the Clean Fifteen.

THE DIRTY DOZEN

The 2016 Dirty Dozen includes the following produce. These are considered among the year's most important produce to buy organic:

Strawberries	Spinach
Apples	Tomatoes
Nectarines	Bell peppers
Peaches	Cherry tomatoes
Celery	Cucumbers
Grapes	Kale/collard greens
Cherries	Hot peppers

The Dirty Dozen list contains two additional itemskale/collard greens and hot peppers- because they tend to contain trace levels of highly hazardous pesticides.

THE CLEAN FIFTEEN

The least critical to buy organically are the Clean Fifteen list. The following are on the 2016 list:

Avocados	Papayas
Corn	Kiw
Pineapples	Eggplant
Cabbage	Honeydew
Sweet peas	Grapefruit
Onions	Cantaloupe
Asparagus	Cauliflower
Mangos	

Some of the sweet corn sold in the United States are made from genetically engineered (GE) seedstock. Buy organic varieties of these crops to avoid GE produce.

Appendix 3 Index

A

almonds 53
anellini pasta 18
arugula 44
asparagus 21, 44

B

baby corn 61
bacon 21, 33, 34, 35, 42
basil 11, 13, 18, 26, 34, 41, 44, 46, 59, 61
beef 7, 25, 27, 29, 30, 57
bell pepper 26, 48
black beans 12, 54, 56
broccoli 35, 39, 53

C

carrot 8, 12, 15, 19, 20, 23, 33, 40, 46, 47, 48, 57
cayenne 15, 38
cayenne pepper 38
cheese 11, 19, 25, 26, 29, 32, 35, 46, 51, 54, 57
chicken 7, 17, 18, 19, 20, 21, 22, 23, 26, 32, 34
cinnamon 15
coriander 12, 13, 18, 26, 37, 38, 41, 54, 56
corn 47, 54, 61
cumin 18, 26, 34, 54

D

dandelion greens 48

dried basil 34
dried sage 47, 61
dried thyme 11, 13, 15, 27, 28, 29, 30, 32, 39

E

egg 19, 23, 41

F

feta cheese 60
flour 13, 19, 32, 35, 46, 51, 60
fresh basil 18, 26, 44, 46, 59, 61
Fresh basil leaves 26, 44, 59, 61
fresh dill 40
fresh parsley 7, 8, 9, 23

G

garlic 7, 8, 9, 11, 12, 13, 14, 15, 17, 18, 19, 21
garlic cloves 11, 13, 14, 22, 34, 41, 54
green beans 61
green curry 38, 61

H

haddock 39, 53

J

juice 13, 15, 20, 22, 39, 40, 58

K

kale 48

L

lamb 26, 28
lemon juice 15, 39, 40, 58
lime 13, 20, 22, 38, 54, 61
lime juice 13, 20, 22

M

milk 18, 32, 38, 39, 45, 48, 50, 51, 53, 54
mushrooms 8, 45, 50
mustard 33

N

noodles 19, 23, 38, 41, 48

O

olive oil 11, 12, 13, 14, 15, 18, 23, 25, 26
onion 7, 8, 9, 11, 12, 13, 14, 15, 17, 18, 19, 20
onion powder 19
oregano 17, 22, 30, 46, 60

P

paprika 15, 34
Parmesan cheese 11, 25, 26
parsley 7, 8, 9, 11, 23, 26, 32, 33, 39, 47, 51

pasta 18
potato 32, 33, 47
potatoes 19, 20, 25, 27, 32, 34, 39, 40, 42, 44, 51, 52

R

red pepper flakes 58
rice 17, 19, 48, 56

S

salt 7, 8, 9, 12, 14, 15, 17, 20, 21
soup 7, 8, 9, 11, 12, 13, 14, 15, 17, 18, 19, 20
soy sauce 20, 56
sugar 22
sweetcorn 20, 39, 52

T

thyme 7, 8, 11, 13, 15, 25, 27, 28, 29
tomato 13, 17, 26, 29, 41, 46
tortillas 54

U

unsalted butter 32

V

vegetable broth 12, 14, 15, 25, 28
vegetable stock 11, 12, 33, 34, 37, 38, 40, 41, 46, 47, 50

W

white rice 56
white wine 39, 41
Worcestershire sauce 25

Sharron B. Malec

Printed in Great Britain
by Amazon